GOD SPEAKS TO ME IN SILENCE

A BOOK OF POEMS

JANET CLINE

ARPress
ILLUMINATING IDEAS.
EMPOWERING VOICES.

ARPress
45 Dan Road Suite 36
Canton MA 02021

| Hotline: | 1(888) 821-0229 |
| Fax: | 1(508) 545-7580 |

Ordering Information:
Quantity Sales. Special discounts are available on quantity purchases by corporations, associations, and others. For details, contact the publisher at the address above.

Printed in the United States of America.

ISBN-13	Paperback	979-8-89356-858-5
	eBook	979-8-89356-859-2
	Hardback	979-8-89356-884-4

Library of Congress Control Number: 2024909040

Contents

In the Panhandle

The top hat of Texas
Is filled with sand, sun, and horny toads,
Pheasants stride through fields of maize.
Massive thunderheads bring slanting rain,
Fearsome lightning, and the occasional twister.
Sparse but hardy grass in springtime turns green
Then browns off in summer as every living thing
Pants for rain.

'Neath the sleepy mesas,
A roadrunner runs express train-like, speedy but silent,
Across the dry-cracked plains. A rattlesnake slithers
Through low-cut ruts in an unpaved country road.
A meadowlark sings from a twisted cottonwood tree
That draws from a near-dry, weed-choked creek bed.
A dust-devil swirls, recalling dust bowl storms
Of other days.

Chin Up

Racing through war-torn London,
Watching pilots' dog fights overhead,
Sleeping in blitz-proof shelters,
The years of her girlhood fled.

She married her American soldier,
And held a girl child to the light,
Then she tackled a brand-new country,
Trusting God to make it right.

Alone now, she greets the future;
"Chin up, chest out" her watchword true.
With pluck and courage she looks forward
To seeing the final chapter through.

In honor of my British "Mum,"
Elizabeth Safford,
August, 2006

The Legacy

If one's dad, whom one adored,
Read voraciously, rapaciously,
Devouring words like apples, enjoying every bite,

Would not his daughter follow after,
Chew through books and crooks – gadzooks!
Relishing plots like diamonds, as imagining took flight?

A reading dad's a treasure,
What a legacy, ecstasy – philosophy, he leaves!
Better far than pots of gold – the key to literary sight.

In memory of my reading Dad, Don F. Safford Jr.
Written 2006

Boredom

Boredom…
Saps intention
Traps the Soul
Zaps the Spirit

So LIVE…

Fare in Zeal
Care with love
Share in gratitude

Old Friends' Voices

Old friends' voices – dear friends' faces,
Come to us at Christmas,
Life gilders, love builders,
Memories grown so precious.

Stop in time a moment now.
Recall our love and laughter.
We'll hold you in sweet regard
Today and ever after!

Older than Dirt

When you're older than dirt
And your bunions hurt,
When you've gone past your days
And your innards are ablaze,

That's when you're most apt
To snarl, grumble and snap
At those who try hardest
To give you their best.

Remember this and temper all
When dementia comes to call,
For love is the sweetest wave
To carry with you to the grave.

Temptations

The Miracle—

Turn these stones into bread

Bread, I've been dreaming about bread.
At first it was meat, rich and red with blood.
Now the thought makes my stomach cringe,
After 40 days, any meat is too rich a food.

Is it really so bad to turn stones into bread,
To slake my own hunger with a seedy bun?
I could do it, Father, I know the Power in me,
The freedom You give us makes it harder to shun.

Mankind won't understand my eschewing miracles,
When the tricks that I scorn would help me to live.
Yet I understand, I know "Man doesn't live by bread,"
My own comfort, my own body, I must give.

I refuse.

Temptations

The Mystery—

If Thou Be the Son of God, Cast Thyself Down

High I stand on this turret, all the world stretched before me;
A leap would be so easy, would the angels come nigh?
Would they bear me up, take loving charge of me;
Would I gain their succor from on high?

The voice—the Voice, I hear inside, outside, all around me,
Prove you are the Son of God, it says, Prove it or die!
It is written—it is written, you have their protection,
All the world will believe in you if you but fly!

That's not God's way—the magic, the mystery, the tricks;
Not my Father's way to gain love by bending the rule.
Life is a blessing, love the heart's precious treasure,
Faith alone the fathomless, priceless jewel.

Don't tempt me!

Temptations

The Authority—
All This Power Will I Give Thee

I am dizzy; my head spins as I stand on this mountain;
Thoughts of power and glory more dazzling still;
Don't we want this world to worship us, Father?
Wouldn't it be easy to win them with our skill?

I could do it, Father; I could win them all for you.
All it needs is fashioning the kingdom they want,
And ruling, not unkindly—think! No wars, no bloodshed;
It would be so much easier, their sinfulness to daunt.

Dizzy, my head's clearing, Father, what am I saying?
Take away free will, free choice from your creation?
Love, love by choice, is the way to the kingdom.
Every man (and every woman) has his own revelation.

Begone, Satan!

Written after reading the chapter, "Temptation, Showdown in
the Desert," in Philip Yancey's book, The Jesus I Never Knew.

Courage

Courage, it's said,
Is daring to try again tomorrow.
Is that how it was for Mary,
The days after Jesus was born?

Arising, heart-whole,
Anticipating God-only-knows.
Wonder-full at the shepherds' song,
The sages' precious, exotic gifts.

Setting off, heart-fearful,
To escape mad Herod's wrath,
Fleeing with Joseph to a foreign land,
Little knowing the child's full destiny.

Sore perplexed, heart-broken,
To see her son at Calvary;
Courage, is daring, so they say,
To look with faith to tomorrow.

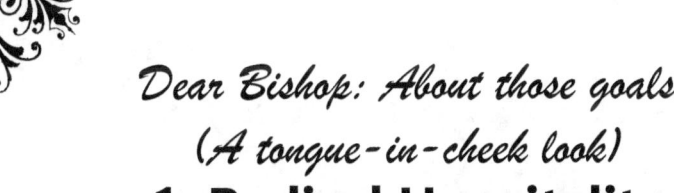

Dear Bishop: About those goals
(A tongue-in-cheek look)
1. Radical Hospitality

Radical: such an odd thought to tack onto Hospitality
-- A word that smacks of genteel manners, a smile
Of earnest good will, a cup of coffee, perhaps,
Offered in a china cup, chatting all the while.

Why Radical? Does hospitality need something more?
More – say – than Let me hold the door for you?
Than Let me show you to your seat, or, Find your coat,
Smiling friendly-like, pleasant through and through?

Radical hints of strangeness, of surging overboard,
Outside self-taught limits, of crossing boundaries
Of courtesy, of stepping, as Jesus did, across the line,
(The one that divides us,) to love the least of these.

Dear Bishop: About those goals

2. Passionate Worship

And another thing, Passionate worship, can we do that?
Is it proper in a culture rife with lust?
Surely we should worship God politely,
Not stimulate ourselves farther than we must.

Should we really get all that excited?
Should our music be that fervent and strong?
Heartfelt prayers can be so embarrassing,
Heartfelt testimonies go on much too long.

If we engage in Passionate worship,
Our children might get caught up on a whim
They might even fall in love with Jesus
And waste their lives following him.

3. Faith-forming Relationships

Now, I've really no problem with this one,
My church friends are the dearest I know;
They'd come to my aid in a moment,
Their faces Sunday mornings are aglow.

The Relationships I've formed are wonderful,
We have Faith in each other, it's true,
God's love binds us all together,
It's a shame others don't fit in, too.

4. Risk-taking Mission & Service

Here we go again, linking Risky mission with gentle service,
Surely if we serve our church and its members with grace
That should be enough, a significant outlay of time given
To a pleasant, really deserving sort of place.

But mission, I don't know, that's a concept
That speaks of going places foreign and strange,
Perhaps across the world, war-torn and hungry,
Perhaps across the tracks to hope to change
-- The unchangeable --.

Risk-taking, that's a frisky phrase
For something that's really quite dangerous.
I don't know if I could do that, not really,
It's out of the question, isn't it? -- downright treacherous.

5. Extravagant Generosity

So, suppose we give our money like we've always done.
We'll even dig deeper to the core.
Generosity, that's surely the ticket,
Or does Extravagant mean something more?

You talk like it's really quite possible
To meet that challenge you unfurled —
The one of making disciples of Jesus Christ
For the transformation of the world.

(Honest, Bishop, it was written with tongue-in-cheek.
I really embrace your goals whole-heartedly!)

How can I do less?

Jesus opens his arms to me,
Loving me through all the mess,
The chaotic strain I've made of my life,
How can I do less?

Loving acceptance is the key
To healing in the midst of stress,
Receiving gladly each human soul,
How can I do less?

Receiving with willing heart each new day
Learning all people, all life to bless,
Gaining power through Jesus to redeem,
Wrapped in love, how can I do less?

Keep me, Lord

Keep me alert, Lord.
Someone needs a phone call
To boost their spirits.
I'm the one who can make it
Let me not fail to pick up the phone.

Keep me on track, Lord—
Aware of the priorities;
Friends outweigh in importance
So many trivial things.
Let me be a friend in all ways.

Keep me awake, Lord,
To the opportunities around me,
To the blessings that are mine;
So that when you come in guise
Of friend or stranger, I'm at hand.

My Friend

My Friend, I'm only wondering
As I ponder your schism from this family
If you're expecting, perhaps, a little more
Than mortals can provide;

If your search to find the perfect church
To meet your beliefs, your hopes,
Is futile, beyond the bounds of able-ness
That we simple Christians hold.

If in leaving our open-minded, open doors,
You may find other doors harder to crack,
Other theologies harder to swallow,
Other companies less accepting.

No, we're not perfect, far from Christ-like,
Often less than loving, filled with pride,
Yet we hold you in our hearts' eyes,
And always we wish you well.

Shepherds

We were just poor shepherds,
Scraggly, low-life know-nothings
Who lived in the fields above Bethl'em
Following the woolly-tails.

That's how we're made,
Us shepherds, somewhat mean, fiddle-headed,
Yet soft enough with the animals,
The tiny lambs, the mums, even the rams.

But the tale I meant to tell you
Was not about us, no more about the herds,
It's a night tale I can hardly tell you,
Hardly whisper, for I don't know the words.

There was a man (or not a man),
And he appeared-like, just popped up on the hill,
And seein' us shaking, said not to fear
But be joyful, for his news was wondrous.

He told us of a king new-born,
Nearby, in the hills, to poor folks like us,
And he—well, he glowed, shone so strange,
And his clothes glistened, too, like new snow.

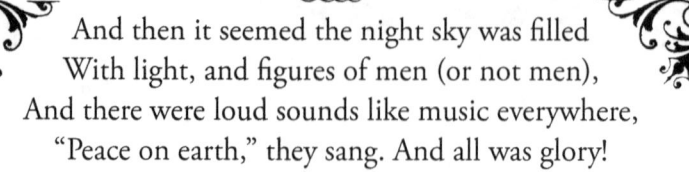

And then it seemed the night sky was filled
With light, and figures of men (or not men),
And there were loud sounds like music everywhere,
"Peace on earth," they sang. And all was glory!

Oh, I can tell you, we cowered there for a spell,
Then gaining strength, we rounded the flock
And took off for the cavern in the hill, you see,
Where the heavenly phantom said the child lay.

And he was there in a trough, such a tiny thing,
With his mother sitting by and his dad round about
Seeing to the animals, and it seemed almost like
The child shone, too, like the sky-men who told us.

And it was sacred-like, the time we spent there,
Kneeling rough in the dirt before him,
With his mother smiling the while and seeming
About to say something, and his dad brooding by.

We left after a while, and stumbled back down the hill
And found the sheep where we left 'em, grazing quiet.
I've told the story many times, respectful-like,
But I wonder, yes, I do, What's to become of this babe?

--December, 2006

Pledge from An Open Heart

I will remain—
Heart open, hands open,
Willing to help as I can,
Willing to give all I can,
Lord, help me be willing.

I will remain—
Ears open, arms open,
Ready to listen if I'm needed,
Ready to give hugs as I'm needed,
Lord, help me be ready.

I will remain—
Eyes open, life open,
Looking for truth—Your truth,
Seeking for answers—Your answers,
Lord, help me be compassionate.

— 2005

*With thanks to a prayer quoted by the Dalai Lama in his
book, An Open Heart.

Traces of Grace

Rough-hewn shepherd, awe-filled, befuddled,
Wizard on camel's hump, star-struck now,
Fearful young mother, resolute, courageous,
Traces of grace touched every brow.

Small stooped Zacchaeus, whining, grasping,
Stately Arimathean, playing a secret part,
Swarthy thief, dying, crying out in agony,
Traces of grace touched every heart.

Modern-day sinners, seeking a Savior,
Sophisticated "Christians," shunning the poor,
Saints and rogues together, redeemed, forgiven,
Abundance of loving grace opens wide the door.

-- 2003

Broken Angels
(For Lynn)

God sent a little angel to live in your house,
To laugh and grow and prosper in your care;
But angels are fragile and sometimes they break;
So it was with Rhonda – as her illness rare…

Stole away agility and understanding mind…
Made it hard to walk and work and speak coherently,
But you persevered and taught her and brought her far,
And God filled her loving spirit abundantly.

When you answer for the things you've done
In the realm where God and Christ and Spirit rule,
Make no mistake, your golden crown will be --
You loved a broken angel and made her your jewel.

Value Added

A marriage can go two ways as its years progress,
Life for each partner can go stagnant or digress
Into separate paths that bounce off an invisible wall,
And seldom cross in purpose or meaning at all.

But, diversity in marriage can become a stronghold
As each partner contributes to a pattern so bold
That value expands through each one's addition,
And each one gives all to an inestimable mission.

So it is with my friends on this golden anniversary so fine,
Through skills in learning and healing, they outline
A foundation of love and laughter, as each reflects
On a "value-added" marriage of worth and respect.

— 2007

Ray and Lyn

With so much love and laughter,
So many memories and good times –
You cobbled together a marriage
That was filled with upward climbs.

Your love of your faith is paramount,
Your children a part of that grace.
Organizational skills and humor
Met every difficulty you had to face.

And now you have come to the pinnacle,
You've reached that landmark golden day;
Enjoy the great fruits of your labors,
We who love you are with you all the way.

-- Janet Cline, Nov. 25, 2011

Dear Departing Pastor

I think I'll remember you as an unsettling force –
Overly emotional to some,
Too often long-spoken to others.
But to those of us who stuck with you,
And those new ones who flocked to you,
You brought so much of hope,
So much eagerness to serve,
So broad a sense of mission,
And ministry, and service.
So wide a swath of lovingkindness
You carved through our defenses,
Joy broader than a hurricane,
Building, never breaking.

I think I'll remember you as an unsettling force –
Who caused those who would to change and grow,
Who carried us forward and up to new heights,
Unsettling as Christ was, and filled with his purpose.
I'll remember you with gratitude and love.

2008

For A Friend

You are so sure, so very straight and strong,
Sometimes we who love you forget things can go wrong,
That you ache for the child who's struggling so,
And your days flow over as expectations grow
From everyone around you – but most of all your own,
As you strive so hard to master the service of God's throne.

But God still girds each day with gracious love and care,
God knows your anguish, makes each challenge easier to dare.
When things are spinning 'round you at a dizzying pace,
Sometimes brokenness can move you to a higher place.
Prayer and song are natural talents to restore a joyous soul,
And keep you moving forward toward a glorious goal.

July 2007

Kathy

She's a strong combination:
This woman of East Texas,
Pragmatic, common-sensical,
But heart-warm and soul-deep
In serving Christ's mission.

She talks to young children
In a way that's part schoolmarm
And part co-conspirator,
Yet heart-warm and soul-deep.
They love her exceedingly.

She's her husband's staunchest ally,
And stands steadfast behind him
Stalwart-fine and loving;
And heart-warm and soul-deep,
She supports his ministry.

She's a loyal friend to turn to
In joyfulness or perplexity,
She captures the essence of ideas,
Ever heart-warm and soul-deep,
She's there for you always.

-- 2008

Clark Gardens after a Thunderstorm

On the lake a tall heron stands motionless, a sentinel,
Stunned, perhaps, by the furor of the night before.
Further down a swan swims in grateful peace and silence,
Ducks and geese venture forth to preen along the shoreline.

Debris clogs the pools and litters the pathways
As weary but willing workers ply rakes and leaf blowers.
The roses – Daydream, Apricot, Julia Child – are bedraggled,
Heads broken, petals blasted by the wind, the hail, the rain scourge.

The chapel sits quiet, thankfully spared by nature's wrath,
While at the station house, toy trains circle gaily through tunnels
Designed to delight and entertain the youngest, the oldest, too,
And tables, wiped dry, provide welcome rest after walking the trails.

Though damaged, the gardens are still a work of beauty,
The paths laid out in imaginative, labyrinthine splendor;
Of treats for the eye, sites for meditation and dreaming,
Wondrous scents wafted forth from a wealth of different flowers.

The storm was fierce, ferocious, frightening,
But the roses, larkspurs, azaleas will blossom forth again.
The paths will beckon invitingly to all who come here,
Clark Gardens will thrive once more.

--By Janet Cline, May, 2013

The Year of Rita
(September 2005)

Hurricane,

A force we'd never felt before
Knocked us for a loop
Left us shaken and disturbed,
Far from home, disoriented.

Winds of Change,
Yet we found hope and kindness
In far-off churches,
With folks and friends and new friends,
Cell phone stay-in-touch calls, caring.

Destruction,
Homes and trees every which-way,
Our church left crippled,
But when we gathered to worship again,
God heard and mended hearts' wholeness.

And Advent comes,
With promise of Christ's coming,
We prepare for the child,
The gift and promise of Bethlehem,
Heals us to sing and praise once more.

Here We Are, God

Here we are, God
Seeking to find a purpose
For lives lost in trivia,
Games of chance, fine apparel,
Diets and drivel.

If we put half the time, God
Into searching the sad eyes
Of folks lost in loneliness,
Kids in need, men in trouble,
Moms exhausted,

Chances are we'd meet you, God
As we found our purpose
By helping each hungry stranger,
Each hurting friend and coworker,
We'd find our souls.

-- 2004

Journeys

Journey
To see a kinswoman
Sharing of secrets
Inner leap
Joy.

Journey
To Bethlehem on business
A donkey, an inn
Weariness
Joy.

Journey
To Nazareth with a baby
Secrecy, terror
Escape
Joy.

Journey
Through Advent for us
Remember a babe,
A cross
Joy.

Multitudes of Joy

And suddenly there was with the angel
A multitude of the heavenly host,
Praising God and – yes -- singing
With their joyful, tuneful most.

Whenever I take my favored place
Near the end of the second row,
I, too, sing with joy-filled heart --
Joined with other spirits all aglow.

We may not be a chorus of angels
As we sing of the Christ Child's birth,
But we sing with heart-full rapture,
And we're filled with a glorious mirth.

So, when you hear a church choir singing
Of the birth of the King of Kings,
Remember that choir of angels
As all our glad spirits take wings!

Do you hear what I hear?

Do you hear what I hear?
Is it bells or a lullaby sweet?
An angel chorus or a baby's cry,
A song or a bird's glad tweet?

This song of joy will fill the earth
If humankind can but hear,
This night holds a promise of infinite worth,
This birth is a cause for great cheer.

Come, listen with hearts wide open,
Come, worship the child foretold,
Hear the good news he brings us.
What a marvelous gift will unfold!

-- 2009

Traveling

It was not a good time to go traveling
With the baby coming and all,
But we still felt a stir of excitement
As we went to obey Caesar's call.

Traveling means new sights and people
With more than a hint of dangers,
But the time to give birth was very near,
Time for closeness, not for strangers.

Traveling meant that my Joseph
Had to leave his carpenter's trade
And for our families back at home
The Chanuka feast was delayed.

It was not a good time to go traveling,
Even the donkey felt the strain;
But he persevered, as did Joseph
As we traveled together in twain.

Traveling meant trusting the Lord again
With the holy birth impending.
Traveling meant reaching with grateful hearts
For the mean hospitality extended.

A grotto for animals stacked with hay
Spelled the end of traveling and travail,
I gave birth to my son 'mongst silent beasts
And we praised Yahweh of Israel.

Reunion

What happened when I saw you again?

We hugged and my eyes
Sought to rediscover the child
Mapped in the adult lines of your
Strange-familiar face.

Then I listened for a sign
In your voice, your laugh,
Your not-saids,
That that child still lived,
(Older, yes, and wiser)

The child I loved and played with,
And tried on selves, and styles,
And grown-ness,
Like Mom's old flowered hat.

Then, when the child peeped out
Through time's fingers,
Bright-eyed,

My heart sought evidence of your now-state,
Loved ones, faith, well-being –
Proof God had drawn your plan,
If not easily, then well;
Given you tools, strength, Far-sight,
How beautiful – the fulfillment of you.

-- Janet Cline, July 25, 1993

New Year

Refresh.
The new year is upon us,
Splash in the waters of hope.
Step forth, clean with purpose and clear of eye,
Into this new day.
Plunge into the ocean of opportunity
Serve, spend your talents.
Be joyful.

Hold fast to the rope of determination.
Clutch it! Don't let it go.
Grow strong in the Spirit;
Refresh,
Renew,
Be reborn.

Frances

Dearest friend of my childhood,
Decades later, miles apart, still my friend…
Each of us married our great love,
Yours was whimsical, fun-loving,
Mine more studious, dreamier;
But both marriages "took."
We are blessed that way.
We both had loving children
Who grew up fine and honest.
Your 50-year golden marriage
Carried you in later freer years
To far-off campgrounds, nearby lakes,
But always together, You and Bob,
What a blessing
To love and cherish
Each other's company!

-- 2011

Carol of the People

I, said the businessman in suit of grey,
Carried His message every day,
I spoke words with love, the compassionate way,
I, said the businessman in suit of gray.

I, said the homemaker holding her child,
Gave him my babe so meek and mild;
And offered to train him right all the while
Into a Christian without deceit or guile.

I, said the teacher, straight and tall,
Hold his promise close as I give my all –
Teaching the young ones and answering my call,
I, said the teacher, straight and tall.

— 2000

Homeless Man

Trudging wearily
Down the road,
Homeless man,
Heavy load.

Homeless but
Still at peace,
Ringed with friends,
God's release.

Bound for a cross
Content to die,
Homeless man—
Heaven's nigh.

Fear Not...

I send you a babe –
Not a fearsome ogre,
A dragon, a soldier –
But a child.

I send you a savior –
Not a dreadful scourge,
A striker, a purge –
But a healer.

I send you a sign –
No nightmarish fiend –
But a lover, a friend,
An example, a teacher,
A gentle outreacher,
A child.

Fear not.

-- 1998

Prepare for the Coming

"Prepare for the coming of Christ:"
That's our task for the Advent moon,
But what does it mean to prepare
For this day that is coming so soon?

Shall we pray to use Christ's approach
In all we endeavor, say, show or endeavor?
Shall we prepare by lifting our hearts
Out of the humdrum into a glow

Of Christ-like love, true Godly caring,
As we reach out to each fellow and ma'am?
Will "Prepare" become real in our hearts
As we struggle to follow the Lamb?

Shall we try to improve each encounter
With a loving, helpful resolution?
Shall we honestly seek to surge forth
To a God-blessed, heart-felt solution?

"Prepare for the coming of Christ:"
It's a Christmas-like challenge to take
From the flame of a hill-side manger
Into each life for Jesus' sake.

A Poem for Advent
(after 9/11, 2001)

Then an angel of the Lord stood before them, and the glory of
the Lord shone around them, and they were terrified. But the
angel said to them, "Do not be afraid..." Luke 2:9-10a

When fear crashed in,
We had to remind ourselves
Constantly not to be afraid.
Cataclysmic events shook us to our very roots,
Toppled us like tall towers, disoriented
Our thoughts, our actions, our theology.

When 3,000 souls were lost,
Taken in a blinding, fire-filled moment,
We trembled crying at
The enormity that clapped this evil thunder,
Triggered war and pestilence and pain
But bloomed in flags, in songs, in unity.

Fear not, the angel
Still reminds us, staunchly
Standing tall and cold and awe-full,
Night sky blossoming and burning round him,
Sounds like music soaring, muting all the clamor
Save the tinkling bells, a child's cry, restoration.

The Road to Redemption

The road to redemption can be crooked indeed,
With many a pothole of pride and of greed.
You may twist an ankle,
Aches and pains may rankle,
But travel on with Jesus and from his word feed.

For He'll lead you safely beside waters still,
You'll find you are growing in grace and good will.
Walk on sturdy and strong,
Find within you a song,
For he has redeemed you, your heart he will fill.

We celebrate two births at Christmas:

There was the birth of a child to a maid and a man
Just an ordinary babe, many must have thought;
Except for some shepherds, star-struck by angels
And so-called wise men, addled by their journey.

Yet we praise that birth more than two centuries after:
That "ordinary" babe destined to be our Savior;
And those shepherds it seems had it right all along,
And the gifts of the wise men rightly went to a king.

But there's another birth we herald, Peter's Gospel says,
Another "babe" who's born in our world today;
For in his mercy WE are born to living hope and promise
By the life and death and triumph of Jesus o'er the grave.

Treasures

Gold and precious spices the wise men bring
To the tiny Christ child whom they rightly deem a king.
Their gifts were precious treasures it is very true,
Yet more precious by far was the child himself
And the gifts he bore for humankind – for me and you.

A tiny babe in a stable rude lifted his arms that night,
Blessing shepherd and king alike as they came to see the sight
Of one born to spread his treasures throughout the earth,
Mapping a path of love and joy and peace forevermore,
No cross could destroy his Way, foreshadowed at his birth.

A chance to live quite honestly, righteously, with love,
To serve mankind a new way, while seeking God above.
To cherish the poor and "the different" as our kinfolk all,
To sacrifice sin and pride and arrogance to him alone,
And find forgiveness and salvation as we hear his call.

It's ours as we embrace it, this treasure most precious of all.
It's ours, it is ours indeed. Worship the gift in the stall.

— 2010

Dark Night of the Soul

Agony wracked him,
Trembling washed him through,
Enervated his wiry strength
As fearful images drew
Him deeper into horrors
And darker into pain,
He fervently longed to run and hide:
What could his death gain?

The garden's heavy scent
Threw him gagging to his knees,
Crying, he reached upward,
And pleaded, "Father, please…"
Heavy sweat poured bloodlike
Down his furrowed brow,
He asked again, "Please, Father…,"
But knew the answer now,

Stood and straightened slowly,
Eased his aching spine,
Stepped clumsily, then firmly,
And now there was no sign
Of doubts and fear and shaking
That weakened him before;
He strode on to the cross and death,
Renewed in his spirit's core.

-- 2006

Christmas 1997

As six planets align in the still, cold night,
Glowing, unblinking, a marvelous sight,
It seems the dear Father has seen our plight –
Blank-eyed kids with guns, homes cast asunder,
Amoral "heroes," havoc caused by man's blunder –
It seems He is sending his message of wonder,
(Much as He did on that other starlit hill,
Over a manger, hushed, waiting until ...)
"Fear not, I love you, I'm with you still."

The Strong Heart:
Community Unity

The strong heart that drives our city
Has been hidden quite a while;
Its beat is overridden by
Shouts of cantankerous bile,
And arguments, and rancor,
And internecine strife,
We need to pull together
And share blessings of life.
Then the beating of that strong heart
Will calm and cool the fears
And make us one in hope and love
And soften all our years.

Unless Ye Become...

The eyes of weariness
Gazed up from a careworn world
And saw only night.
The blackness of war, and grief, and pain,
Then the eyes of MAN looked down again.

The eyes of confusion
Turned hopefully to the skies
And saw clouds and yet the sun.
These eyes found joy in living, yet shed many tears,
The eyes of YOUTH looked onward, bravely, but with fears.

The eyes of purity
Looked up from whimsical play
And saw – the trees, the butterflies, the buzzing bees.
The soft, gentle rain was just another toy,
And the eyes of the CHILD laughed – with joy!

-- 1964

Why?

"Why did we go?" you ask me.
Well, there was this star!
Brilliant above all others;
And it seemed to beckon
Night after night it called.
We spoke about it, the others and I,
And decided we'd have to go.
You say "wise men" now,
But they called us fools.
The way was long,
Our backs were sore,
The camels were testy,
But still the star beckoned,
Still we went on.
We knew not of the babe
We'd find when we got there,
Knew not of the challenge
That was coming to the world,
The child who would forever
Change the future.
We knew only of the star
And God's call.

— 2012